DEDICATION

To my three magical children,
Tyson, Calvin, and Faith.
May the world become brighter
because of you. Believe in your magic!

My Magical Words
The Magic of Me Series

www.authorbcummings.com

ISBN: 978-1-7325963-4-4 (hardcover)
ISBN: 978-1-7325963-5-1 (ebook)

Library of Congress Control Number: 2019900568

Illustrations by Zuzana Svobodová
Book design by Zuzana Svobodová, Maškrtáreň
Editing by Laura Boffa

Printed in the USA
Signature Book Printing

First printing edition 2019.

Free Kids Press

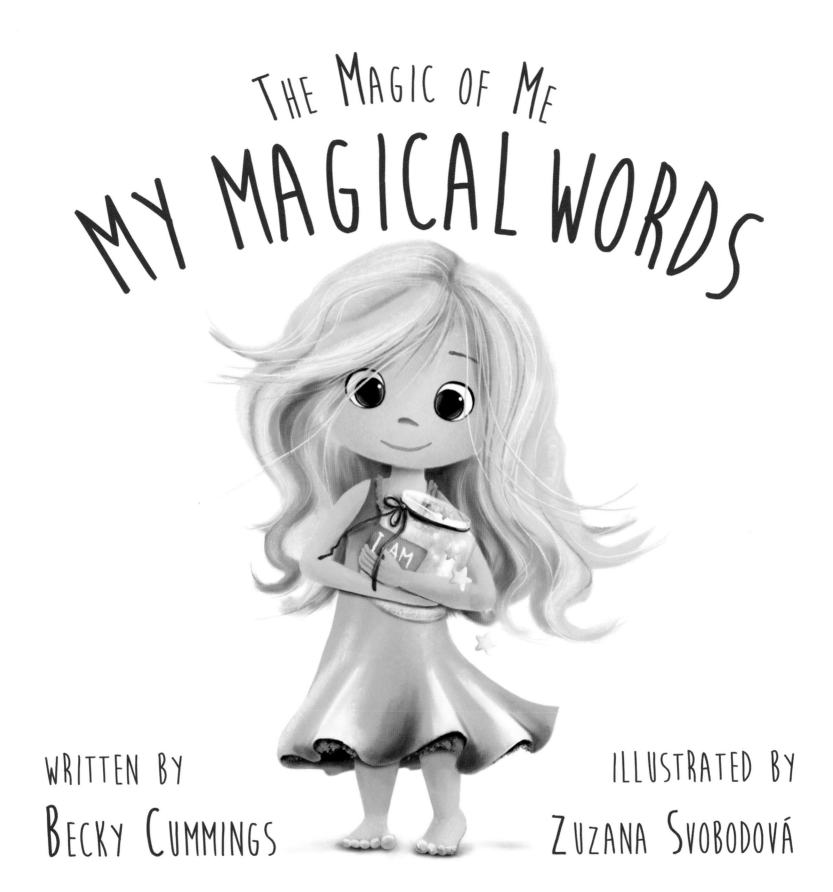

The Magic of Me

MY MAGICAL WORDS

WRITTEN BY

BECKY CUMMINGS

ILLUSTRATED BY

ZUZANA SVOBODOVÁ

The words you speak have super powers!

They can bring sunshine or rain showers.

So here are some magical things you can say,

to bring the sun and light up your day!

Listen closely to this life advice.

Start with, 'I am' and end with something nice!

The more you say these words, the more they come true.

So, repeat them quite often, because

THE MAGIC'S IN YOU!

I am special!

You are a masterpiece, one-of-a kind,

created perfectly with an eye for design.

From your hair, to your toes, to the way that you speak,

all of these differences make you UNIQUE!

I am giving!

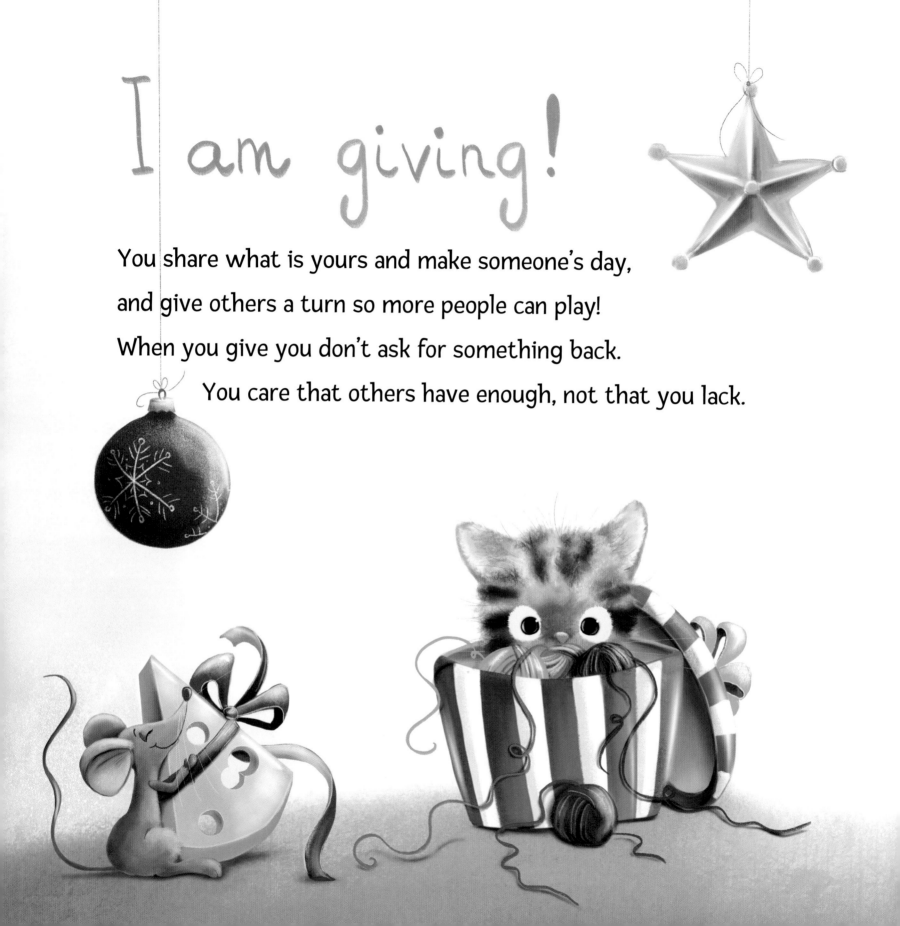

You share what is yours and make someone's day,
and give others a turn so more people can play!
When you give you don't ask for something back.
You care that others have enough, not that you lack.

I am peaceful!

You know how to slow down, relax, and rest.

You know when to find quiet to be at your best.

When it's not time to be loud, but you want to shout,

sit down, close your eyes, breathe in, and breathe out.

I am kind!

You use your voice to say nice words.

You lift people up like wind under birds.

You don't use your words to offend or tease.

You give compliments, you say

THANKS and PLEASE!

I am loved!

Just by being yourself, you fill people with joy.

You are a special girl or boy!

People love you for the many things you have to share.

You are surrounded by people who care!

I am smart!

You listen and learn from the people you love.

Sometimes you look within or above.

It's fun to learn all of the things YOU CAN DO.

Then you are able to TEACH OTHERS TOO!

I am strong!

You run, you jump, you play all day.

Your bones and muscles shout, "HOORAY!"

They love the daily exercise.

It makes them want to

DOUBLE IN SIZE!

I am healthy!

You eat vegetables and fruits galore.

You drink your water, but wait, there's more!

Even though sweet treats might taste YUMMY,

you don't eat too many because they're bad for your TUMMY.

I am thankful!

You are grateful for what fills each day,

like the people you love and places you stay!

With gifts that you get and the fun things you do,

you always remember to say,

"THANK YOU!"

I am happy!

You laugh so hard your belly shakes.

You smile so wide that your cheeks ache.

You lift others up when they feel down,

by spreading your

JOY ALL AROUND!

I am proud of myself!

You always try to give your best.

When you work hard, you pass the test.

You can do it... You did it! HIP-HIP-HOORAY!

You try new things and learn every day.

I am beautiful!

Inside and outside your beauty shines bright.

You glow with love like the moon in the night.

True beauty comes from your heart deep inside.

It sneaks out and pops up, on your smile so wide.

You can be anything you believe.

So say, "I AM" and be ready to receive.

May all your precious dreams come true,

now that you know

THE MAGIC IS IN YOU!

SPECIAL AS CAN BE

THIS IS THE
MAGIC OF ME!

YOUR PICTURE HERE!

TIPS FOR READING WITH CHILDREN

- Have children repeat the positive affirmations after you.

- Create an action to go with each positive affirmation. For example, have children flex their muscles when they say, "I am strong!"

- Ask children to give other examples that show the positive affirmation. For example, after reading the page about kindness you could ask, "What are other ways you show that you are kind?"

ENJOY MORE BOOKS IN THIS SERIES BY BECKY CUMMINGS!

for older readers 8-12

www.authorbcummings.com